hearts apart

juveria

notionpress.com

INDIA · SINGAPORE · MALAYSIA

ISBN

Paperback 979-8-89519-805-6
Hardcase 979-8-89632-387-7

1

Another year,

Another three six five days,

Another eight seven six zero hours,

Another five two five six zero zero minutes,

Another three one five three six zero zero zero seconds

And unlimited moments of your beautiful existence in the world and my heart;

Happy birthday.

2

To this boy sitting on his knees and promising me the whole world,

Can you bring him back to me?

3

Oh God, I pray to you,
Don't exhaust my emotions in mere imagination,
Let him return for real.

I have decided to continue trusting you,
Maybe someday, you will be tired of breaking it,
Maybe someday, you will feel bad about it,
Maybe someday, you will no longer enjoy it,
Maybe someday, it might no longer be feeding your ego,
Maybe someday you will trust in whatever I ever said.

5

I surely am high maintenance,
The Dyson airwrap,
The Gucci bags,
A cake from London's famous patisserie,
A BTS concert ticket;
I demanded none of these feeble things
but your time.

6

The mathematics of love failed me;
I added him to my dream routine
And it trigonometred my whole existence.
I multiplied expectations
And it returned as abstract algebra.

The dictionary needs to come up with some words;

A word to describe the feeling of being handicapped while looking at the world winning races in front of your eyes,

A word for people marrying their childhood love in front of betrayed people,

A word for loved children in front of she-is-strong-she-can-handle girls,

A word that cries, begs to God, crumbles on the ground, and digs itself a grave.

8

Today, for my love, from my death bed, the only thing left to say to you:

I surely lived a happy, content life with all your pain.

Let's meet again when the world would be a castle of love.

9

Hey, you are alone; it's time you find someone to rely on,
You are ageing, and you have to have a partner for old
age's sake,
Hey, come on, say yes to anyone who proposes,
Bro, give yourself another chance;
You will find somebody better
You are left on the shelf.

Babe, I stood through all these tantrums and people.
Aren't you proud of me?

10

During the last third of the night, when God has promised
to answer every crying eye with what it desired,
I pray that my eyes don't bleed with the pain you gave.

11

I don't know if I am loyal in love
Or stupid in life.
I don't know if my heart is broken
Or bored.
No idea if feelings are real
Or if it's adrenaline.

12

I can't leave you stating, "I shall leave you for your happiness."

A moon, a sunshine, a billion stars,

A galaxy of happiness, all I have kept wrapped for you,

So, stay back and buckle up. You are in a spaceship to the pink paradise.

13

The place next to me is filled with emptiness, space just as much as you left;

How are you expecting anybody to fit into a shoe torn by you?

How are you asking me to move on while holding the most hurting nerve of me?

How shall I see you in someone else's eyes when I lived years blinded by you?

14

Why aren't we together?

I guess he missed imagining holding hands and walking
on a beach.
I guess he skipped imaging waking up next to each
other every morning
I guess he thought 'it's okay, it's a mere heart affair'
Ummm, I guess maybe he just
didn't love me as much as I loved him.

15

Ideally, forgetting him would be equal to forgetting what
love feels like
Or maybe what it feels like to feel a thing;
How do you diss the presence of the heart while alive?

16

Don't just pop up one day and ask me how I am doing;
It's not possible to note down every piece of death felt.
Don't just come on that day when I gave up my last hope;
It's just not possible to rise from the grave once laid.

17

However, all said and complained, I love you;
You connect me to the farthest mile on the earth,
You connect me to the distant heart filled with love.
I will keep my ring finger blocked and
My surname space empty.

18

Was I running towards you while you were running away from me?

Was I chasing you while you were chasing something else?

Was I delusional about a life with you while you were climbing reality?

Was I being a fool while you were just enjoying your 20s?

Was it just me hallucinating about true love while you were gimmicking the same?

Was I just a part of your life while you were my whole existence?

Was I only touched to the skin while I felt our souls tangled eternally?

Hey, was it ever 'Us' or just 'You' always?

19

I need eye contact with you;
I have so much to complain about,
I have so much to show you around,
I have so much to make you feel,
So much to remind you of,
So much to ask you again,
So much to make you believe,
So much to tell you regarding,
So much to promise you,
So ...
So much more,
One eye contact.

20

There was supposed to be light at the end of the tunnel,
I see gloom everywhere.
Tricked again to believe they cared
I hear the devil's laughter everywhere.
So long and so dark to find a way back;
I smell betrayal everywhere,
You did it to me yet again
I feel left worthless everywhere.

21

The stains on my soul are evidence of how I was killed;

I was stabbed with unending longingness and dragged into pitiful sludges,

I was made to drink pretty poison and said to have been loved a lot,

I was strangled with a flower rope and was iterated the fear of losing me,

I was burnt with rose petals and told to be the most beautiful girl,

I was cut into pieces with hidden disloyalty and patted to be the most patient one,

I was kept alive for the love of sadism and said to be most cared about.

22

I'll wait a million lives for you,
Just promise me that you'll be back;
Without any complaint without any hesitation I'll be patient.
I'll enjoy waiting dreaming all that you and I will do;
Just come back once, even if it is to leave again.

23

That guilt of breaking an innocent heart will never let you live in peace;

All the tears embedded in her pillow will become a sea to drown you,

The nights when she was awake missing you will come to haunt you forever,

The prayers she did for your success and comeback will turn into curses,

But the love she has for you will just be love unconditional.

24

To
The last chapter of my book,

We failed to make it a saga.

Yours,
Missed Opportunity

25

To a big mansion-heart

A name meaning to spread happiness

A shy, cheerful red-headed girl

Who was like the love between the setting sun and the
shining moon

And the world ended up making her a

decaying happy virus.

26

The nights are getting colder and tougher,
I've tried all sorts of heaters and easers,
The darkness in my room gets darker;
I've switched on a ton of lights,
The room is empty and way too quiet.
I've played the loudest of music and put the greenest of plants and nothing changed,
There needs to be a way out of all this,
There needs to be you coming back home.

27

Need an eraser for the year 2023;

It drew regrets and a spoiled future

For the sake of my mind and sanity,

A 20-thousand-year sleep for the lost nights,

A hole in the brain that leaks overthinking,

Backspace to cried over moments and a restart to the memory game.

28

The urge to manifest you even subconsciously and dream every night,

To wake up next to you sleeping and wondering if it's real

Every imagination comes true and urges me to let my face show all that happiness,

Walking around with you unashamed and with a named relationship,

The urge to upload pictures with you and just write cheesy captions below them,

Pray the night behind you and get zoned into looking at you while you talk,

Fighting with these urges needs to be awarded, too.

29

They say dreams can be interpreted

Well, can someone interpret what it means to see a long road with a person on a horse at the end of it?

You've been running, running out of breath, running fast, running, focusing at the end of the road, running determined of it.

The seasons have changed, the years have changed, and the directions of the wind have changed.

And you haven't reached an inch closer to the Prince.

30

Still missing that last eye contact,
How much I wish it lasted longer,
Waving hands at each other, bidding goodbye,
Unaware of it being the last one.

Still missing that last eye contact,
How it had no words but a screaming silence,
Giving spine-shivers looking at each other,
Unaware it meant the pain of parting.

That last eye contact is now an everlasting reminiscence
Reminding of joy, peace, and satisfaction being lost.

31

On my way to discover the feeling of a loved person

How does it feel when someone pats your head smiling at you?

Puts their hand on your cheek to comfort while feeling you are in pain,

Looks at you with love, noticeable by everyone surrounding,

Walks along with you, as slow as you, while you wear high heels,

Turns back and extends his hand to make you cross a not-so-big mud puddle,

Nudges you to the inner side of the road while talking casually,

Falling asleep on their shoulder and them not moving till you wake up;

So much to discover, so much to feel - with so much distance in between.

32

I've shared the secrets of my sneaking out of the house at midnight and clubbing;

All of those boys that me and my friends have pranked on Instagram,

The way I stole money from dad and told obnoxious lies to my mom,

I've seen the mole behind your ear and the one in your eye, too

I've known the texture of your hair and the smell of your cologne,

I've breathed the warm, long breaths of yours

Felt shivers from your touch and went numb every time we were together.

Is there a way we're closer than this?

33

God, I need a memory waiver;

If not that, throw me into the past,

If it's time for me to come back, let me carry all I want from the past,

If I can't carry all I want, let me look at everything closely once more.

34

Petitioning for salary pretending;

It should have the highest of packages,

Pretending to look at things unaffected,

Pretending to sleep to avoid your own thoughts,

Advising friends on relationships, pretending you had a perfect one,

Pretending to love without a drop of oxytocin;

Every level would make me a millionaire.

35

Delusion

Feeding my delusion with a day

Sitting with my friends at a cafe

Receiving a call from you after a decade

Asking me to turn back and, to my amaze

Seeing you dapper in a white shirt wave

Oh, my delusion. I turn back, fall on my knees, and cry

The hug that I waited for forever.

36

Happy new year

Entering the new year without you

But still with you.

An ocean of hope still stands there, dumped with last
year's baggage.

37

I'm still there
Maybe not a call away
But just a late reply away.

I'll always take care of you
Maybe not by being there when you are sick,
But by praying for you irrespective of times.

I may still trouble you
Maybe not by saying my intrusive thoughts out loud,
But by deranging your thoughts between busy hours.

I'd be there even if you were not there.

38

Hey world, maybe it's too soon to say this:
Maybe I never deserved something like this,
But now it's time that I get a peaceful sleep,
I have no will to wake up and work hard,
I have no power to fight destiny anymore.
Let's part ways for some time, and I'll be in your loving memory forever.

39

The thing about you that I love the most:

You being an awkward potato amidst anything,

Being shy when our eyes met, signalling that we both have the same thought.

Scrunching your nose at things I'd say to tease you,

Setting your hair a zillion times between conversations,

Your scent.

You.

Every time I see you, I have a constant smile on my face,
Every time you held my hand, I wanted to glue it there,
All the times we've spent together, I wished to stop it there.
I really ended up being in love with an amazing person;
I won.

41

I started writing you mine
And people called it poetry.

42

I have been lately thinking about how much I miss you,
I think about you in every moment of my day,
There was a point when we were together the whole day,
And now there is this time when I miss you the whole time.
Later, all this missing will also just be a memory
Turning moments into memories tonight, too.
Missing you tonight, too.

43

Today, on the praying mat
When I finally made up my mind to ask God to turn my
love away from you
All I could think at that time was
Even if I wanted to
I wouldn't be able to hate you.
So, ended up asking to return you to me again.

44

2 years 3 days, and a few hours after
The flight that left Seven Seas far
I meet a lot of people,
Nobody feels like you.
Even after 30160 flights coming back without you,
I still wait.

45

This time, when I catch you in my dreams
I will hold you a little tighter,
I will try not to wake up,
I will follow you in the light; you disappear,
But if I blink and come back from that world
I will not give up on this dream.

46

I have written a book on you
Started my book with
I wish...
And ended it with
To be continued...
Titled it my *Unending Desire*.

47

All that you need to measure my love for you
Is to know that, even without you
I am yours.

The only fear I withhold in me
Is that on the day of judgement,
When I ask God
Why my prayers for you were never answered,
And God replying to me,
"Because he never asked for you."

49

All my courage,
All my strength,
All my trying, my will,
All my 'I don't miss you' anymore;
I've moved on
Stand shattered by one glance at your picture.

50

I will not believe in setting your love free, and if it's yours,
it will come back;
I will not leave you till the end,
I will not let you go, be it whatever,
I will not be the girl you will come back to,
So if you ever go...
Don't bother coming back.

51

A sad song that was released a decade ago,

Sung at every occasion,

Loved to the core but never understood;

Or maybe the lyrics never felt,

Is now my life analogy.

"Har dua me shamil tera pyaar hai,"

"Bin tere har lamha bhi dushvar hai."

52

I don't think I can find love again;
Your footprints in my heart
Are a bold sign 'no entry'.

53

Seeing crowds and so many faces
Holding hands and giggling people
No one's alone, but no one's talking
Turning my head to you, my only reason
To be belonging to this era.

54

I know, for a change that
My tears have no value
If they did, I'd have pillows worth million dollars.

55

Would it hurt you too?
Realising that it's 2024
And you are still processing 2018.
6 years of living on a cloud
Fearing the burst but loving the high.

56

You were all the trends on Instagram
Even before they started trending,
My alpha,
Red flag,
Pasandida Mard,
The LOML.

57

I definitely have so many pictures of you;

I know how you sound,

I know how you'd look talking,

I have your answers to all my questions,

I have imaged hours-long conversations,

I have given reactions to your compliments and anger and whatnot;

But my heart

Still wants a rendezvous with you.

58

Have you forgotten
You are my property?
Remember: I sealed with osculation
And put a stamp on you with a

59

I knew that he would go;
He knew that I loved him beyond reason.
But he still stays
And I'm still trying to leave.

I wonder if I made enough space for myself in your heart,
Tomorrow, if I die, I'll at least be alive there.

61

When everyone was applauding for me,

When I was winning in life,

When I was making a home on Cloud 9,

When I was smiling cheek-to-cheek

When I got everything,

My eyes were searching for 'My Everything'.

62

Calling each other with cringe nicknames
Deciding the names of our kids,
Drawing the house we would live in,
Signing random papers and calling it marriage,
Behaving like typical husband-wife,
Vibing to B-grade Bollywood love songs;
Everything is worth experiencing with you
No matter how cliché that sounds.

63

My eyes have accepted that you have left
The abode, the garden in my heart, a stamp on my
memory, a numb lost girl, and her world
And here's my heart still refusing to accept this goodbye.

64

Can life be like that?
The him and the me
Right before my alarm rings.

65

From asteroids to the 21st century,
The dumbest thing to exist on earth
Is a woman in love.

66

If I ever turn my back on you
Just remember you always have a chance to stop me,
And I will always have the chance to show you what you
had done to me.

67

Hey, all you need to do is feel the way you felt when we met the first time,

The rest all will fall in place.

All you need to think is we will see whatever happens later,

The rest all will fall in place.

All you need to know is the planner of the plans will take care of everything,

The rest all will fall in place.

68

Everyone is expressing love in different and beautiful ways;
I had no choice but to be silent.

When you were near me,

My hands never shivered,

My eyes never knew anticipation,

My stomach never felt butterflies leaving,

And my brain is never a pessimist.

You held my hand,

You looked into my eyes,

You gave butterflies,

And you gave me dreams to live for.

70

I did not fall in love with you on day one,
I was brought closer and closer, every deed by deed,
You built and built the expectations higher
Showed me flamingos during sunsets,
And kissed me in public.
You were my Roman Empire.

71

I never understood why you would suddenly ghost me for
weeks.

Why would you just keep saying you are busy,

Why stop me from being hopelessly romantic,

Why meet me in a hurry always.

Though, now I understand well

These smaller doses of poison were to develop immunity.

72

Don't exhaust yourself playing football on weekdays,
Don't just leave the house on an empty stomach and
empty pocket,
Get the broken nails checked by the doctor before they
turn serious;
Take care of yourself
You are not in my prayers anymore.

73

The brunt of us deciding to part ways

Has left our daughter sad more than us;

She had to come to the world to be your favorite,

Her name will now remain on the tissue paper alone,
forever uncalled.

We'll have one less fight to decide who she resembles,

She deserved a better ending.

The two eyes of yours and the two eyes of mine
The most tired battle they fought,
Two won, and the two never picked the sword.

75

The fact that our relationship does not have a socially accepted name
accepted name
Bothers me at least 1440 times a day, once every minute.

# 76

Above all, chaos in my mind,
Late-night mood cramps,
Unwanted turmoil of feelings;
Besides so much missing, wanting, praying
It always feels like something right is happening.

I'm working hard to keep myself busy,
Not meeting people to avoid conversations
Silencing social media and my phone for mood swings,
Living life far from the edge for the fear of falling and still
being alive.

The 'excuse-o-meter' for a mindset of never moving on:
running low
Needs an upgrade.

78

The reason behind my happiness might be beautiful,
But the reason behind my sadness is worth all the beauty
of happiness.
It gives me reasons to never give up,
It gives me reasons to be stronger than yesterday,
It gives me wings to fly higher than the ability I gauged.

79

People who have had all the luxury
Treat love as a can of worms.
Awkward to be in it
Embarrassed to leave it.
I am a worm out of that can.

80

Painting forever in the era of situationships,

I've chosen a difficult path for myself:

Either a forever gets painted, or a situation destroys it all.

81

The waves of missing you
Sometimes hit the shore loud and destructive;
At other times, peacefully swap away the grains of
adrenaline gushing.

82

They say it takes a lot of courage to speak;
I learnt it takes a lot more to keep quiet
And a hell lot when the heart is full of questions.

Funny how I keep recalling
You asking me what's wrong
My what's wrong asks me what's wrong.

84

The conversation is serious,
The complaints have piled up,
You come with a generous lifetime's time.

85

It might look difficult, maybe tormenting to love from far, but for me

Every day is a new day in love,

Every day starts from the first meeting feels, ends on the last handshake.

Every moment is falling in love to rising to the victory moment,

I love you immensely.

86

This morning where there was sickening glory of future
and a calm silence of the past,

Yet again I chose to stay in the calm,

Yet again I chose to be silent,

Hence choosing to be yours, all over again.

87

Love in silence,

Just like the wound that heals over time,

Just like the blade that turns dull over time,

Just like the waves that become calm at some point,

Just until that pain fades,

Let me love alone.

88

People not understanding,
People pointing fingers,
People mocking the differences,
People being judgmental;
Let's hold on to each other even if it hurts.

89

Liars are people who say time heals all wounds,
I can swear on time that it's just fancy talk;
The one who suffers, suffers all alone,
My scar was once wound and now cancer.

90

Hey, my crush

I love you 24/7, 365.

Not in a mood to cook, just order now. Aren't you bored? Watch this new addition to your favorite genre.

Made a compilation of your photos from a year back, would you like to see?

All the things I've ever wished to hear from you are now thrown as mere lines from vita, Zomato, Amazon and Google pics.

91

I had to let go my strongest emotion and my most beloved person

At a time when I was rising and shining I had to choose to hibernate,

And forced to become a tearless hurt baby left alone in the pram on a cold night,

All cause my destiny decided to have the last laugh.

92

A place today reminded me of you,
A fight we had made me tear up,
A down in memory lane held me again,
A loss I gained made me silent again.

93

My delusion,
I hated how much power you had over me and how much
I loved it at that time.
To be ruled over and ruled by you, for mere dopamine.

94

One sided love has been called many names:
Beautiful, painful, incomplete, truest;
I found it to be a heaven that I curated
Soul'ey.

95

The cover page of my book,

The wallpaper of my phone,

My Whatsapp dp and Instagram story,

I've put a black curtain on them since,

You said to keep 'us' a secret.

But I terribly failed,

They question why I am mourning.

96

The rhythm of my soul,
It's a rhythm that's constant,
Never skipping a beat;
It's like a symphony
Playing in my heart.
So I'll keep dancing to this beat
With you by my side.

97

Worse for me is all that I had to write,
For the sake of myself,
The way I loved you.
What's worse for you
All that has happened
Or all that could never happen of us.

98

You'll call it a storm the day you read these lines, but
remember
You ruined the calm in me;
For a day like today, to call me insane.
Till the time you reach here with all your sanity
It'll be my turn.

99

I hate mere imaginations, come live with me;
I'm hanging on the edge, hope you'll save me,
I'm waiting for you, wish you would surprise me,
I haven't removed the ring, yes marry me,
Accompany me and come live with me.

100

I had come to return you the ring you put on my finger
not meaning anything,
You shouldn't have looked at me with that smile which
meant everything to me.

101

It's better to write a horrible book
Than a lovely suicide note.